First published 2017 © Kenzo Benjamin

Text: Kenzo Benjamin

I0157123

Illustrations: © Seth Juelz Ndaba

The right of Kenzo Benjamin and Seth Juelz Ndaba to be identified as author and illustrator respectively of this work has been asserted by them in accordance with the Copyright, Designs and Patents Act 1988.

ISBN 978-0-9931361-1-5

Ignish Publishing House. UK

TABLE OF CONTENTS

CHAPTER 1

STADIUM MADE BY CHILDREN

When I was six years old in 2012, Olympic Games were held in my country, UK. It was a great time. My family mostly watched the games on television. One afternoon, my parents took me to watch the athletics and field events at a stadium.

The place had many people and there was a lot of excitement. From where we sat, I could see most events. There were large TV screens high up so we could not miss anything. People were cheering the competitors. We could also see the blue sky. The weather was lovely and sunny. I

had a glorious time. There were   many different flags of different countries being waved. Mum bought me a British flag which I was waving. I had an ice cream in the other hand which I would forget to lick when there was a racing event. The stadium was full. I waved as athletes from my country were running past. It was all very exciting and electric. There were people selling ice cream, burgers and fruit. The children sitting next to me were eating chips and burgers. They had Jamaican flags and were wearing the Jamaican flag colours.

There was a lot of excitement and cheering when the athletes were running, jumping, throwing javelins. Many people were taking photographs and others were shouting competitors' names or the name of their country. I looked at the shape of the stadium, the seats, and the roof and fell in love with how it was built and how many people it housed during the games. When we left, I wanted to be an athlete who builds stadiums when I grow up. For many weeks I talked about this visit. I drew and coloured many stadiums in my sketch book.

I showed my grandparents the sketches and we would discuss the practicalities of building some of the sketches. Grandparents showed me how some of the designs I had might not work.

I used clay to build little stadiums in our garden on the lawn during my free time. I was fascinated with the construction of stadiums. I even used sticks to build. I would place some of my toys on the seats to represent people sitting in the stadium. My dog, Gigi, always broke the stadiums I made to pieces as he thought I was playing a game. I never got tired of starting again.

Two weeks after the Olympics were over, on a sunny day, I went to the beach with my parents, grandparents and cousins.

We were building castles on the beach and splashing in the sea water. I had a sudden flash of inspiration to make a

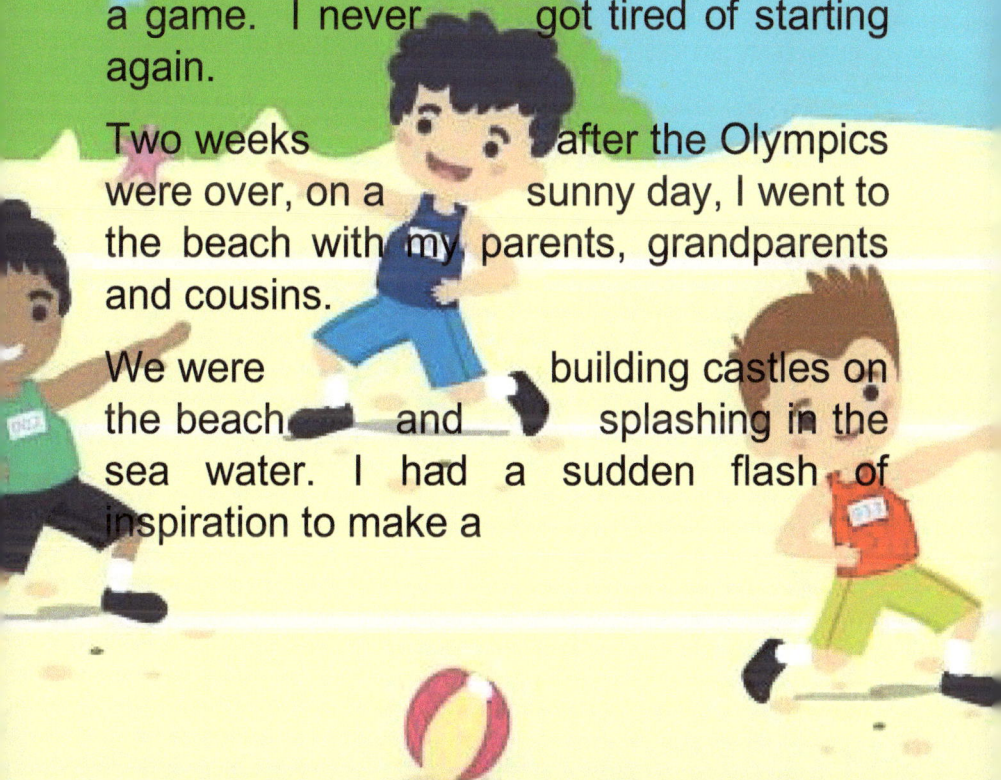

stadium. I persuaded my cousins to work with me to construct the stadium. Soon we were bringing many buckets full of sand to a large open place on the beach to make the stadium. We made a large semi-circular structure with three stepped places to sit on. We used our toy spades to firm the structure. We were working so well together that soon other children joined us to complete the stadium with more buckets of sand. Within a short period of time, it was a huge structure.

Some of the older children helped to shape the stadium properly. Cousin Warren's dad wrote at the top of the stadium, 'Sunny Stadium.' We were all very proud of our work. We persuaded parents and grandparents to sit on the stadium steps under their umbrellas. We all sat on the steps and had our lunches, mostly fish, chips and drink. Many people told stories of the recent Olympics and their athletic achievements.

I learned a lot of interesting facts about competitors of the last actual Olympic games. Some children started asking their parents why they had not participated as competitors. Ruko's father told us that he used to be a 100m athlete but he had injured his knee, 'Otherwise I would have won a gold medal.' His family nodded and smiled. He encouraged us all to join a sporting activity at school to keep fit and maybe compete internationally. We started playing hide and seek. A lot of toddlers had fun hiding behind parents or at the back of the stadium. There was a lot of laughter.

Many of the toddlers were hiding in almost open places but those my age always made surprised looks when we found them. They would giggle away, find another place to hide and the game continued. Cousin Wayne's dad sat us all down on the steps of the stadium and told us about some of the greatest athletes from past Olympic Games. He made us believe that we could also do great things.

Warren, who was seven years old, challenged us all to a race. He said, 'We have made a stadium, we have many children here who can run and jump. What are we waiting for?'

We all looked at each other and suddenly realised that we could really do this. We took up the challenge. Warren's dad drew the finish line in front of the stadium. My dad measured about 50m from this finish line to the start line near the sea water's edge. We drew the track lanes in the sand. That alone was fun, trying to get the lanes to be parallel. Ade's father bought a whistle, some poles, a tape measure and a rope for the high jump from the nearby shop.

We put a lot of sand in an area which was going to be used for high jump. The excitement was building up. Parents made sure we all had sun protection.

Chapter 2

THE CHILDREN AND PARENTS' ATHLETICS

We had some 3, 6 and 8year olds running in their own races. Soon a crowd gathered around us, clapping and cheering the athletes. The athletes wore their beach sandals and swimming costumes. Cousin Christopher's grandfather had a stopwatch to time the athletes. Ryan's grandmother was recording the winners' names and the time they took to do events. Sue's grandfather had a loudspeaker, which he used to announce the races and the winners. My dad took his white board from our car and this was used to record the events.

Suddenly events had unfolded and become bigger that I had expected. People, who earlier did not know each other, were working together to make the sporting events a reality at the stadium. My mum

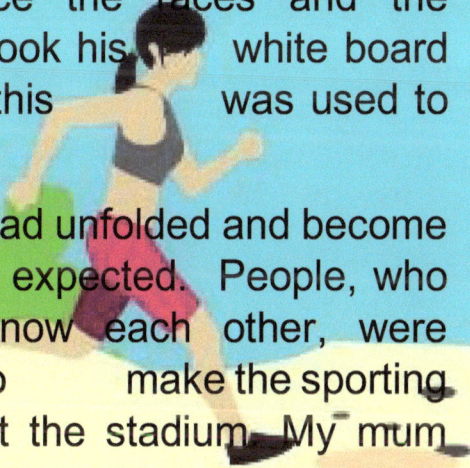

was doing the, 'On your marks, get set, go!' bit and blowing the whistle. The amount of energy that this project had generated was amazing.

This project had now taken on a life of its own with many people volunteering to help. There were some children and parents sitting on the stadium steps cheering us on. Soon many more people gathered to watch or join the sports. I ran in the 6year olds group and came second after a tall boy called Sean. Warren came first in his race against other 7year olds. He made the same sign that one of the Olympic athletes made to show lightning speed.

There was great laughter and excitement as all tried to make the sign. I saw my

parents taking photos of all this. Some children started showing their muscles and jumping up and down to show how fit they were. Many photographs were taken. Some parents had taken video clips of the races.

The race for eight 3year olds was fun to watch. They ran together. One fell and they all stopped to pick him up. That was amazing. Little Ruko won the race. He raised his little arms up as a sign of victory. His parents hugged him and gave him a flag and he was

very excited.

The high jumping event mostly had children aged 8 years old and above. We all cheered as the contestants attempted to jump. Wayne won the race after jumping 70cm.

Soon after the high jump competition, we all tried long jumping with little success for most of us. Afterwards, all the athletes took a swim in the sea to cool down. We then sat on the stadium steps and discussed the sporting activities we had participated in. We had a lot of drinks to cool down. It looked like everyone had enjoyed the events.

I lay on the stadium step and imagined I had built a bigger stadium by the beach and people from all nations were competing in it.

I could hear people cheering in my imaginary stadium. I could hear the commentator saying, 'Just to remind you ladies and gentlemen, that this stadium was designed and constructed by the famous Kenzo Benjamin, the well-known stadiums designer.' In my head, I could hear the applause and could see the newspaper headlines the following day. I saw myself being interviewed about the design of the stadium. I was woken from my dreaming by a sandy beach ball which hit me on the head. Well, so much for dreaming. I was amazed that so much fun for many different people had been generated by my fascination with stadiums.

Liam's mother asked everyone to be quiet and she said, 'Well, the young ones have shown their talents, it is time for the parents' race and then the grand parents' race.'

All children cheered. Parents came out slowly to volunteer for the races. The lanes were extended further to the sea to make them 100m long.

First was the women's race. Only 9 mothers were running. My mum went to the starting line and looked at me as if to say that I should not laugh at her. When the whistle was blown, they ran fast. Little Janet's mother won the race and made her lightning fast speed sign. My mother came fourth. They were all hopelessly out of breath but seemed to have enjoyed the race. They rushed for their water bottles.

Five mothers were doing high jumping. They jumped over 1.3m. Charlene's mother jumped 1.4m. and was the overall winner. There were many tense moments before the jumps. It was fun to watch children cheer their parent on.

The men's race had twelve competitors. We had to increase the lanes to accommodate them. They took their places. When the whistle was blown, they took off. This was a very fast race. The excitement and cheering that followed was unbelievable. Everyone was standing up on the stadium steps.

The race was very tight. Keith's father won by a fraction of a second. He was checking if he had beaten the world record but he had not. His family went to meet him at the finishing line. All the competitors were breathless and sweating.

The men's high jump had 7 competitors. My dad was not one of them. The competitors were all very good at high jumping. Ade's father won. He jumped 1.6m. The tallest child amongst us was 1.10m tall. We were amazed that they were jumping heights like that with ease. Ade's family waved towels and cheered when the father won. We knew that if we trained well, we would also be able to jump that high. As we took down the high jump equipment, we played tug of war with the rope and fell on the sand. It was fun.

We took another dip in the sea water to cool down afterwards. We seemed to have unending energy because even as we took the dip, we raced to see who would swim further into the sea. Soon we were more than 30 m into the sea. Parents called us back. We swam back reluctantly and sat on the beach.

Chapter 3

GRAND PARENTS' ATHLETICS

The grandparents' race was exciting and drew a large crowd with a lot of children in front cheering their grandparents. Some of their adult children were fussing, worrying about their parents running.

Grandmother's race was more like high energy fast walking. Four nans

competed. They walked very fast digging their walking sticks in the sand. Kieran's nan won amid much cheering. Five grandfathers competed in a fast walking race.

Emily's grandfather won. He did a little dance which we all imitated. The grandparents enjoyed participating. Some had their walking sticks and they still fast walked showing determination to win.

I thought this was an amazing cross-generational event which had started because of my fascination with building a stadium. The grandparents did not volunteer to do high jumping. The teenagers on the beach did not want to participate in the races although they helped to set up everything, especially straightening the lanes and getting equipment from the shops. Their contribution made most events possible.

Chapter 4

FOOTBALL

Little Thandie suggested we play football, boys against girls. At first many were not keen. Thandie said, 'Well, if the boys are too chicken to play then girls will just play on their own.'

Little Millenia started making,

'Cluck! Cluck! Cluck!' sound of a chicken and soon all the girls were making the sound.

That was enough to get the boys to agree to play. We arranged for teams of all age groups with 9 aside. All adults chose to watch the match.

We drew line for the football ground and used buckets to mark the goal posts. Leanne was goalkeeper for the girls. Wayne was the boys' goalkeeper. Keith's father was the referee.

We played for 20 minutes and took a 10 minute break and them played another 20 minutes. Both sides got away with many fowls.

Little Millenia picked up the ball with her hands kicking it into the goal post and scored. Hunter dribbled, went off-side and still scored. Some played for 10 minutes and went out saying they were tired. I played for 15 minutes and went out when I was out of breath.

There were those who argued whilst playing telling the other team members not to mark them. The good thing is that no one was injured and in general we all had fun. Wayne had refused to play but he was the commentator and linesman. I was amazed by the zeal he showed making the commentary of how we were playing. His mother was taking a video of him.

By half time, the score was 10 to 5 in favour of the girls. The crowd cheered. I saw dribbling styles I had never seen before. There were boys and girls with dribbling moves and ball techniques that teams would pay a lot of money for. When the

whistle blew, the score was even at 12. We went into extra time which was very tense. This is when the boys won. The score was 16 to 14. We had all enjoyed this football game but it was hard won because the girls put up a real fight. We all felt very thirsty. after the football match and rushed to get drinks.

Chapter 5

PRIZE GIVING

Warrens' dad then announced that it was time for all contestants to receive prizes. We wondered what the prizes were.

We found out later that parents had put money together and Little Samantha's grandmother bought a lot of fresh ice cream cones from the Ice cream seller.

We all went one by one to a makeshift podium to receive the massive ice cream cone, shake Samantha's nan's hand

and have photos taken. There was also ice cream for the 8 teenagers who had assisted us. We all cheered loudly in appreciation of the work that had done for us. Samantha's nan then thanked everyone for their contribution.

The winner of every event got a big ice cream cone with chocolate flakes sprinkled on it. We ate ice cream and drank water or juice.

Afterwards, parents were sending each other the videos of the sporting events on their mobile phones. We looked at some of the videos and shared the viewing. There was much laughter. I did not have a mobile phone. I asked friends' parents to send the videos to my dad's phone.

CHAPTER 6

STADIUM DISAPPEARED. LESSONS LEARNED.

We were all having fun eating chips, chocolates and talking loudly as we sat on the steps of our stadium when someone shouted, 'Look, look, the tide is coming in, soon the sea will destroy our stadium!'

Sure enough, the tide had risen and it was sunset. We had had so much fun being involved in all the activities that we did not realise the time. People started packing to leave the beach. The lanes we had drawn in the sand for the athletics, disappeared. Still the sea advanced towards our stadium, one wave after another.

Parents encouraged their children to help pack all belongings. We also picked litter to leave the beach clean. We said our, 'Good-byes' to the friends we had made. We took more photos together. We helped parents to carry our stuff to the cars which were parked nearby.

Within 20 minutes, a big wave washed a third of the stadium into the sea.

I thought the stadium looked interesting even as it was being broken down by the waves. It had brought together so many different people, strangers who had become friends.

With the next few waves, the stadium disappeared into the sea as its bottom was eaten by the waves. Sunny stadium was no more. It was as if it had never existed. The stadium had brought much fun, love, energy and so much cooperation among strangers. I hope it built good memories for everyone.

In my mind, I could see the children, many years into the future, looking at the photos or videos parents made of this event with pride and fondness. I was amazed that my interest in the structure of a stadium had resulted in a day well spent at the beach with people who many times would not have interacted with each other. People had worked cooperatively to make the events fun for everyone. Some had not participated in any event but they had lent their skill and time for children to have fun.

My family and I had made many friends. We had been invited to many parties by the new friends. The beach stadium had brought a lot of joy to many people and we had shared many stories.

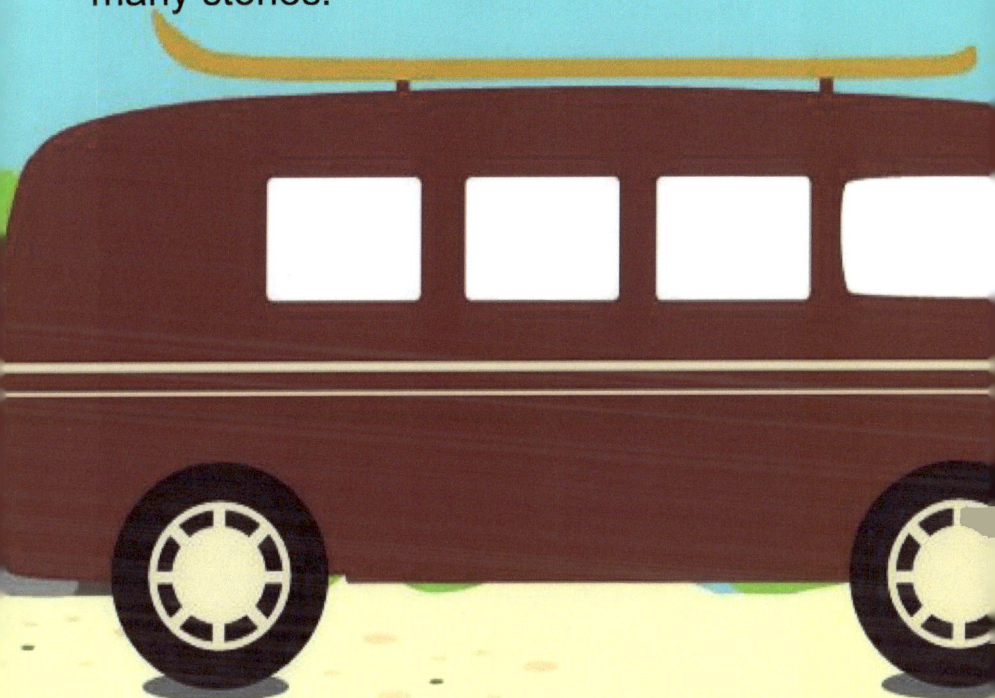

Grandparents had shared stories of their past on the stadium steps and this gave us, children, a lot of useful information.

My granddad had met someone who had been in primary school with him. They had spent the day going over events in their past. Granddad had introduced us all to him and we met his family. Many children made new friends and shared ideas without fighting. We had competed in different activities and enjoyed ourselves.

As we packed our things in the car, dad said, 'Well done Kenzo. We all had a brilliant time around the stadium you and the others built.'

'Thank you, dad.' I said as I put my brown beach sandals into a bag.

Mum looked at me and told me she was proud of me. Nan (Grandmother) said, 'Kenzo, you and all the children built a beautiful stadium. Is that one of the plans in your sketch book?'

'Yes, Nan,' I said.

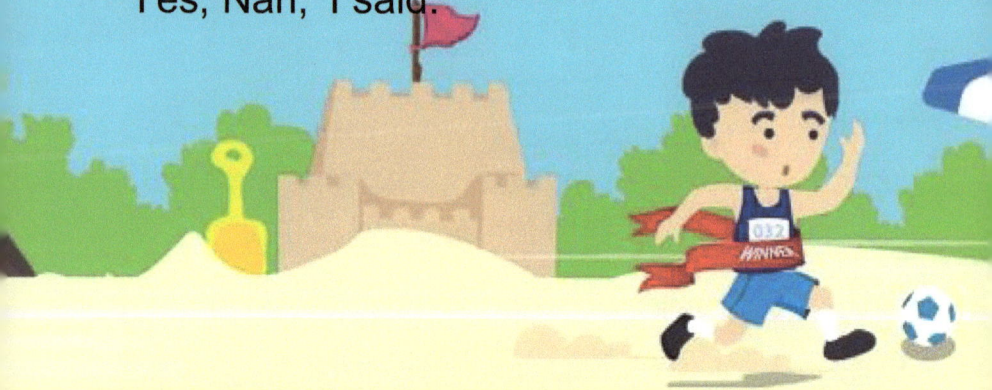

'Planning is great preparation Kenzo. It was also great to see you working so well with other people and accepting their ideas to improve yours. I am proud of you,' said grandfather Stanley. I felt appreciated but I also knew that it was not only me who made the events fun for everyone. All people who were there had contributed to the joy.

'Thank you, granddad. I wish you and nan had participated in the races. I know both of you can run because you run with me when I visit you.' They laughed and promised to participate next time.

I asked dad why he did not run in the race. He said he was talking to friends he had gone to school with and none of them had volunteered to run.

They were also talking about interesting things from their past and he did not want to miss that.

Mum also said she had met people she used to work with and they had shared a lot together. Grandma said it would have been nice to have a barbecue at the end of all events. She had enjoyed it all and was amazed that it was not a planned event but one which started small and grew very big.

We got into the car and dad drove us home.

On the drive, Nan asked, 'So even if you did not come first in your race, Kenzo, what have you learned? Remember, what you learn in all tings is very important.'

'Nan, it was fun building the stadium. I was full of ideas and loved every moment of the races. I learned that working with others makes work lighter and is fun. The older children made the structure look like the steps on a stadium. I learned that others can have ideas that improve what I want to do.

I would have loved to cross the finishing line first in style like that very fast athlete in the Olympics but Sean was running faster than me. I also learned that I need to practise my football skills to play like some of those children. They were amazing.'

Mum said, 'We have videos of all the events you took part in, so you will be able to watch yourself. We have been invited by Sue's parents to come to Sue's birthday party next Saturday. Keith and Ade will also be there.'

'I would love to be at the party,' I said. I was looking forward to that already. I asked for money to buy a present for Sue. Mum said it would come out of my pocket money. I did not mind this. I earned pocket money doing my parents and grandparents garden. I enjoyed being in my grand parents' garden because granddad taught me a lot of things when we were in the garden.

'So, do you want a proper kit for making a model stadium then for your birthday?' Nan asked.

'Oh Nan, that would be awesome!' I said loudly.

'Well, Kenzo, I am sure your wishes have been heard by everyone,' Nan said as she looked at mum and dad, who smiled quietly. She nudged me and we laughed together. I couldn't wait for my next birthday to start building another stadium.

www.ingramcontent.com/pod-product-compliance
Lightning Source LLC
Chambersburg PA
CBHW041807040426
42448CB00005B/302